Micadoo Blue

Printed in the United States of America
Sunny Day Publishing, LLC
ISBN 978-0-9825480-6-6

Acknowledgement

Special thank you to Paws and Prayers for
seeing the potential in Micadoo.

Paws and Prayers mission is to "rescue,
rehabilitate and re-home unwanted dogs and cats;
to prevent overpopulation through spay/neuter;
to restore dignity, trust and quality of life for neglected,
abused and homeless dogs and cats; to find the best
home for each dog and cat in our care;
to educate adopters and our community on pet care,
spaying/neutering, training and suitable animal
selection for their lifestyle; to provide a network of
resources, volunteers and fosters for animals,
animal shelters/pounds and the community".

www.pawsandprayers.org
PAWS & PRAYERS

Dedication

To our family and friends for their love
and support throughout our lives.
To Micadoo for inspiring us
to share your story and passion
for all kinds of people.
And finally, for Tara, your infectious laughter
and fervor for life serves as a reminder
that being different is not a limitation.

— Vanessa and Amanda

I dedicate this book to my family,
and friend Melanie Haren.

— Krista

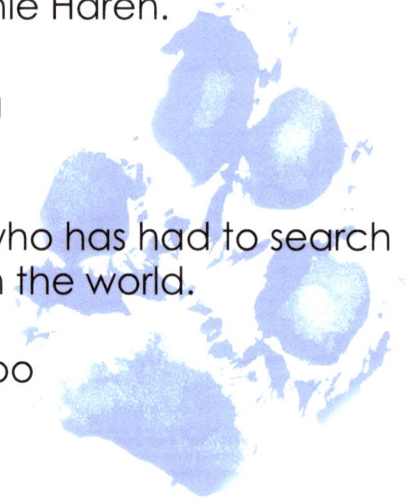

To every person (or animal) who has had to search
for his/her place in the world.

—Micadoo

Micadoo Blue

By Vanessa Ware and Amanda Burke
Illustrated by Krista Stumm

My name is Micadoo, but my friends call me
Micadoo Blue. I'm a Border Collie.
A Border Collie is a breed of dog that is known
for being energetic, friendly and loyal.

Five years ago, I was born on a big, beautiful farm with all kinds of animals. There were horses and cows, pigs and goats, cats and chickens, and even a tortoise!

I come from a family of sheep herders; six black and white dogs that all herd sheep. I have two dog brothers, two dog sisters and two dog parents.
As a puppy, I was different from my family because I was born with a blue-tipped tail. Do you have something that makes you different from other people? Then you know what I'm talking about.

When I got older, I worked in the family business, herding sheep. But something wasn't right. I couldn't herd the sheep; they herded me!
I just couldn't do it right. I felt odd and silly barking at the sheep. That made me very sad.
I always watched my family at work in the fields. They all seemed so happy doing something they loved. I just didn't fit in.

One day I told my family I was going on an adventure.
I knew the farm wasn't the place for me, so I left to find
a space of my own that I could call home.
This is my tale…

After I left the farm, I went to work as a guard dog
at Mr. Lee's junkyard. My first day there I was really
excited! I'm such a curious dog and the junkyard was
filled with so many interesting things. I really enjoyed
walking around the junkyard with Mr. Lee.
He would pet my head and call me, "Good Boy."

When nighttime came, this was a big problem.
It was so dark. It was so scary. I was all alone.
My three nights there were spent with my blue-tipped
tail over my face, waiting for morning to come.
On the fourth day, when morning finally came, I licked
Mr. Lee goodbye and left the junkyard.

I walked and walked for a few days. A nice man at the
fire station called me over and gave me some water.
I was very grateful and very thirsty. He took me inside
and gave me some food and a nice blanket. I laid my
tired body down in the corner of a warm, big room.

The nice man talked to his friends about making me their "fire dog." They all seemed so excited. I wasn't so sure I liked the sound of that. In fact, it sounded hot and scary to me. Still, I was so warm and comfy on my blanket. I dozed off to sleep.

I was awakened by the loudest and scariest sound I'd
ever heard! I jumped to my paws and looked for the
nice men. They were all scurrying about and hurrying
to go somewhere. "Come on, Boy!" I heard one
of them say. I thought I should run away...and FAST!
That's just what I did.

Once again, I was all alone, scared, and wandering the streets. I pondered, "Should I go back to the farm? Should I just give up? Should I keep going?" I was looking for a fun and happy life. I really wanted to find where I belonged. Where was the work I was meant to do? I decided to stop at a park for a rest. Under the prettiest tree ever, I plopped my tired body on the ground and closed my eyes.

I was startled, from my slumber, by a man.
"Where's your home, Boy?" he asked.
I just looked at him with my sad eyes.
He knew the answer.

The dog pound is the place where homeless dogs go.
I was a homeless dog? "I have a home!"
I barked loudly. "You've made a mistake!"
I barked again. No one understood me. I was locked
up in a cage and surrounded by many sad and
scared dogs. All I could do was plop my body down,
close my eyes and go to sleep.

I quickly learned the only way out of the pound was to be adopted. I thought to myself, "Maybe I'm in the perfect place to find a home."
I was calm and friendly to everyone who came to visit the pound. I really love people. But, no one who came to the pound seemed to want me. I was sad.

I spent three long days and nights in the dog pound. On the fourth day, a nice woman with a clipboard came in and took me out of my cage. I was very surprised, but very grateful. "Where will I go next?", I wondered to myself.

The nice lady took me to a place where other dogs were waiting for homes, too. She said I was a good boy and needed more people to see me. This is when I saw Quinn, for the very first time. One look at him and I knew Quinn would be "my boy." One look at me, and with a loud and excited voice he yelled out, "Micadoo!"
I was so happy I barked!

Quinn gave me a new home and a bed. He also did
something very nice. He took me to a training school
to learn how to be a better dog. He taught me how to
sit and lay down. I even learned how to roll over and
not run away when I heard loud noises. I also learned
to stay really still, until he called me. I learned how to
be well behaved and patient around different kinds of
people and in different places.

I was convinced I was just too different to fit in.
I never thought anyone would be able to see
beyond my blue-tipped tail to see who I really am.
Now, guess what? I have the best job in the whole
world, paws down! I get to play with people all day
long. I'm a therapy dog!

The people I visit give me pets and pats, kisses and hugs. I get loved just for being me! I never know what to expect at work. There are people who are big and small, young and old. Each person is different and I love that! Some people have chairs with wheels, use sticks to help them walk and even use their hands to help them talk. My job is to make everyone feel comfortable, safe and happy. Some want licks...some like to watch me do tricks...sometimes they just want to pet me and rub my belly.

I love visiting schools because I get to play with kids, like my boy Quinn. Some of the kids are really active. I teach them how to run and play with dogs, in a safe way.

At the library, some of the children are very quiet and shy. I just lay down while they read to me. It always makes me very relaxed and sleepy.

I also go to hospitals and nursing homes.
The people there are very gentle and sweet. I go
from room to room for special visits and cuddle
with people one-on-one. Can you believe I get
to cuddle as part of my job?

It doesn't matter what each person needs.
They seem to love me, just for being me!
I'm finally happy. I finally love my work.
Being a therapy dog is the best job in the world,
paws down!

herding dog

junkyard dog

fire dog

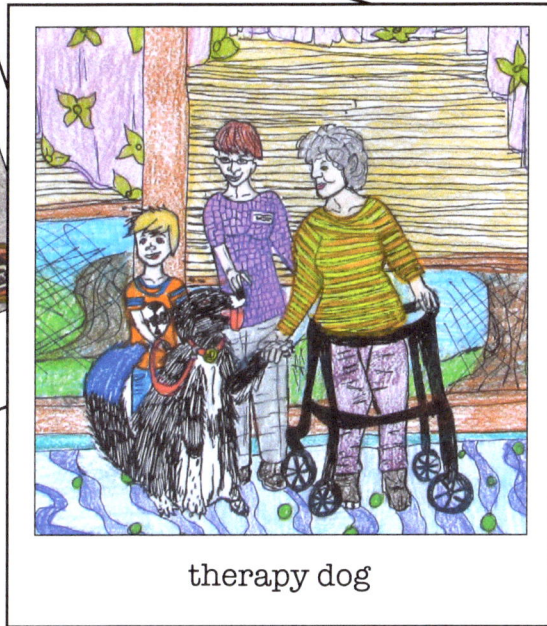
therapy dog

Some dogs are meant to be sheepherders; some dogs are meant to work in a junkyard; some dogs are best suited for fighting fires; and some dogs, like me, are born to be therapy dogs.

At the end of each day, my boy Quinn sings a song he made up just for me: "Oh, Micadoo, Micadoo, with your tail so blue, you make people happy, by just being you!" Then, he gives me hugs, pats, pets and kisses. I'm finally home!

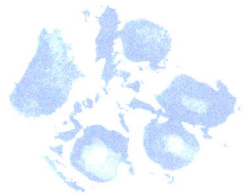

Micadoo is a 6-year-old Border Collie who was rescued from an animal shelter. He loves children, playing fetch with tennis balls, tugging on ropes and being around all kinds of people. He went through special training and took a test to become a certified therapy dog. He is friendly, gentle and loving.

Vanessa Ware

Grew up in Newbury, Ohio surrounded by a menagerie of animals. Vanessa cannot remember a time when she didn't enjoy reading and writing. She is married, and spends her free time volunteering.

Amanda Burke

Native of Cambridge, Ohio. Amanda is a Certified Therapeutic Recreation Specialist (CTRS) and has had the opportunity to work with people of all ages and abilities. These experiences motivated her to co-write Micadoo Blue.

Krista Stumm

Currently attending Kent State University with a degree goal of puppetry and illustration. Krista was born with a disability called Velo-Cardio-Facial Syndrome, and is excited to have had the opportunity to illustrate her first children's book.

www.ingramcontent.com/pod-product-compliance
Lightning Source LLC
Chambersburg PA
CBHW042106040426

42448CB00002B/164